DOGS SET V

Airedale Terriers

Julie Murray
ABDO Publishing Company

visit us at
www.abdopub.com

Published by ABDO Publishing Company, 4940 Viking Drive, Edina, Minnesota 55435.
Copyright © 2003 by Abdo Consulting Group, Inc. International copyrights reserved in
all countries. No part of this book may be reproduced in any form without written
permission from the publisher.

Printed in the United States.

Cover Photo: Animals Animals
Interior Photos: Animals Animals pp. 7, 9, 11, 15, 19, 21; Corbis pp. 13, 17;
    Ron Kimball p. 5

Contributing Editors: Kate A. Conley, Kristin Van Cleaf, Kristianne E. Vieregger
Art Direction & Graphics: Neil Klinepier

Library of Congress Cataloging-In-Publication Data

Murray, Julie, 1969-
    Airedale terriers / Julie Murray.
        p. cm. -- (Dogs. Set V)
    Summary: An introduction to the physical characteristics, behavior, and proper care
of Airedale Terriers.
    Includes bibliographical references (p.).
    ISBN 1-57765-919-8
    1. Airedale terrier--Juvenile literature. [1. Airedale terrier. 2. Dogs.] I. Title.

SF429.A6 M87 2003
636.755--dc21

                                                                    2002074656

Contents

The Dog Family

Dogs and humans have been living together for thousands of years. Dogs were first tamed about 12,000 years ago. They were used as guards, hunters, and companions.

Today, about 400 different dog **breeds** exist. They can differ greatly in appearance. Some can weigh as much as 200 pounds (91 kg). Others are small enough to fit in the palms of your hands.

Despite these differences, all dogs belong to the same scientific **family**. It is called Canidae. The name comes from the Latin word *canis*, which means dog.

The Canidae family includes more than just **domestic** dogs. Foxes, jackals, coyotes, and wolves belong to the Canidae family, too. In fact, many people believe today's domestic dogs descended from wolves.

This Airedale terrier has much in common with other members of the Canidae family.

Airedale Terriers

Airedale terriers are known as the King of the Terriers. They are the largest **breed** in the terrier group. Many people believe that Airedales are a cross between black-and-tan terriers and otter hounds. Others believe Airedales are a blend of several different breeds.

Airedales were developed in the 1800s in Yorkshire, England. They were named for the Aire River in Yorkshire. Long ago, sporting events were held near this river. Terriers were judged on their ability to hunt river rats.

Airedale terriers were originally bred for hunting foxes, otters, and badgers. During World War I, Airedales worked as guard dogs and messengers for the British army. Today, Airedale terriers are common family pets.

Airedales have a strong sense of smell that makes them great hunters.

What They're Like

   Airedale terriers make excellent pets. They are intelligent, affectionate, energetic, and easy to train. Airedales can also be stubborn at times, but they are loyal to their owners. Airedales also make good hunters, guard dogs, or show dogs.

   Airedales get along well with other pets. Airedales can be very strong, but their gentle nature makes them great pets for children. They are also playful and love spending time with people.

   Airedales, like other terriers, have lots of energy. They need exercise every day. Airedale terriers make great companions for anyone, young or old.

Airedale puppies need lots of attention and training to learn proper behavior.

Coat and Color

The Airedale terrier has a **dense** coat that is resistant to dampness. The coat's hard, wiry outer hair lies close to the body and can be a bit wavy. Underneath this stiff hair is another layer of shorter, softer hair.

The Airedale's coat should be trimmed regularly. That is because shorter hair is easier to manage. However, some owners choose to keep their Airedale with a long, full coat.

An Airedale terrier has a tan head and ears. The chest, shoulders, legs, and stomach are also tan. The Airedale's back and sides have a **saddle**. The saddle is usually black in color. However, sometimes a reddish color is mixed in with the black.

The Airedale needs to be brushed often to keep its coat looking nice.

Size

The Airedale terrier is a medium-sized dog with long legs. An Airedale can measure between 22 and 24 inches (56 and 61 cm) tall at the shoulders. This means the Airedale is a big dog compared to other terrier **breeds**.

The Airedale has a strong, muscular body. On average, it weighs between 45 and 50 pounds (20 and 23 kg). A female Airedale is smaller than a male.

An Airedale terrier's head is long, flat, and narrow with a long **muzzle**. It has dark eyes and a beard covering its jaw.

An Airedale often carries its tail high. The tip of an Airedale's tail is usually **docked** when it is still a puppy. A **veterinarian** can do this. It makes the dog's tail even in height with the top of its head.

12

Every Airedale is unique. But they all share qualities that separate them from other dog breeds.

Care

The Airedale terrier's coat needs constant attention. The coat should be brushed at least once a week with a bristle brush. This will keep the coat shiny and healthy. An Airedale's coat should be trimmed a couple of times a year. This will keep the coat from becoming too long and thick.

An Airedale terrier needs lots of exercise. This **breed** needs a couple of walks every day and plenty of playtime. This will keep the Airedale happy and healthy.

Like any dog, the Airedale terrier needs to visit the **veterinarian** at least once a year for a checkup. The veterinarian can check your dog for illnesses and give it shots to prevent diseases. If you are not going to breed your dog, have the veterinarian **spay** or **neuter** it.

Regular trips to the veterinarian will keep your Airedale terrier healthy.

Feeding

Airedale terriers will eat almost anything. However, it is important to give them well-balanced, nutritional meals.

Most Airedale terriers should be fed only once a day. Some people prefer to feed their dog smaller portions twice a day.

Dog food can be dry, moist, or semimoist. Most dogs will eat a high-quality, dry dog food. Others prefer to have some canned food mixed in with their dry food.

Find a type of food that your Airedale enjoys and stick with it. Changes in diet should be done gradually to prevent stomach problems. It is also important to give your dog fresh, clean water every day.

Highly active dogs need more food than inactive dogs. Young, growing dogs also need to eat more often than adult dogs.

Things They Need

Airedale terriers need lots of love and human contact. But they also need strict discipline and training as puppies.

Airedales are very active dogs. They need space to run, play, and exercise. Airedales love to play catch with balls and retrieve objects. Providing them with many different toys will keep them happy. It will also release some of their energy.

Like all dogs, Airedales need a quiet place to rest in your house. They also need something comfortable to lie on. A dog bed or soft blanket works well for this.

Every dog should wear a collar with two tags. One tag shows the dog has had its shots. The other tag shows the dog's name and its owner's address and phone number. A dog can also have a **tattoo** or **microchip** for identification.

Airedale terriers love to play outside.

Puppies

Baby dogs are called puppies. A mother dog is **pregnant** for about nine weeks. Airedales can have anywhere from one to 15 puppies in a **litter**.

Puppies are born blind and deaf. Their eyes and ears will begin working when they are about two weeks old. They can walk at three weeks, and they are usually **weaned** at about seven weeks of age.

Puppies can be given away or sold when they are about eight weeks old. If you are going to buy a **purebred** puppy, make sure to buy it from a qualified **breeder**. Many puppies and older dogs are also available from the **Humane Society**.

It is also important to take your puppy to the **veterinarian**. He or she will give your puppy the shots it needs to stay healthy. A puppy should start getting its shots when it is between six and eight weeks old.

Airedale puppies are curious about their surroundings!

Glossary

breed - a group of dogs sharing the same appearance and characteristics. A breeder is a person who raises dogs. Raising dogs is often called breeding them.

dense - thick.

dock - to cut the tail to a shorter length.

domestic - living with humans.

family - a group that scientists use to classify similar plants and animals. It ranks above a genus and below an order.

Humane Society - an organization that cares for and protects animals.

litter - all the puppies born at one time to a mother dog.

microchip - a small computer chip. A veterinarian inserts the chip between a dog's shoulder blades. If the dog is lost, the Humane Society can scan the chip to find the dog's identification information and owners.

muzzle - an animal's nose and jaws.

neuter - to remove a male animal's reproductive parts.

pregnant - having one or more babies growing within the body.

purebred - an animal whose parents are both from the same breed.

saddle - a colored marking found on an animal's back.

spay - to remove a female animal's reproductive parts.

tattoo - a permanent design made on the skin. An owner can have an identification number tattooed on the leg of his or her dog.

veterinarian - a doctor who cares for animals.

wean - to accustom an animal to eating food other than its mother's milk.

Web Sites

Would you like to learn more about Airedale terriers? Please visit **www.abdopub.com** to find up-to-date Web site links about Airedale terriers, their qualities, and more. These links are routinely monitored and updated to provide the most current information available.

Index